FROM GRANDMOTHER WITH LOVE

From Grandmother With Love

A Life Recalled For My Grandchild

WRITTEN BY JANE PETTIGREW
ILLUSTRATED BY MARY WOODIN

A Bulfinch Press Book
LITTLE, BROWN AND COMPANY
Boston · Toronto · London

First American Edition 1992
Second printing, 1992
Third printing, 1993
First published in Great Britain in 1992 by
Little, Brown and Company (UK) Limited

ISBN 0-8212-1970-7

Designed by Lisa Tai

Bulfinch Press is an imprint and trademark
of Little, Brown and Company (Inc.)

Published simultaneously in Canada by
Little, Brown & Company (Canada) Limited

PRINTED AND BOUND IN BELGIUM

*W*ith love from _____

*T*o _____

*D*ate _____

FAMILY TREE

Father's Family:

Great Grandfather _____

Great Grandmother _____

Great Grandfather _____

Great Grandmother _____

Mother's Family:

Great Grandfather _____

Great Grandmother _____

Great Grandfather _____

Great Grandmother _____

Grandfather _____

Grandmother _____

Father _____

Grandchild _____

Mother _____

Grandfather _____

Grandmother _____

 GRANDPARENTS

My mother's family

My grandfather's name _____

My grandmother's name _____

They were married _____

_____

They lived in _____

_____

Their jobs _____

_____

My father's family

My grandfather's name _____

My grandmother's name _____

They were married _____

_____

They lived in _____

_____

Their jobs _____

_____

Y PARENTS

My father's name _____

Date of birth _____

Place of birth _____

My mother's name _____

Date of birth _____

Place of birth _____

How they met _____

_____

_____

They were married

Date _____

Place _____

After they married, they lived _____

_____

_____

Their jobs _____

_____

_____

photograph of
your grandmother
as a young girl

$\mathcal{I}$ WAS BORN

I was born:

Date _____

Place _____

I weighed _____

My parents named me _____

_____

My parents told me later that _____

_____

_____

_____

_____

My brothers and sisters _____

_____

_____

_____

_____

_____

_____

My Early Childhood

When I was a little girl:

My family lived _____

My favorite toys were _____

_____

_____

My favorite stories were _____

_____

I liked playing _____

_____

_____

I started school when I was _____

My childhood quirks _____

_____

_____

Things I remember about my parents _____

_____

_____

_____

$\mathcal{M}$Y SCHOOLDAYS

My first school was _____

We had to wear _____

My best subject was _____

My favorite teachers were _____

_____

My best friends were _____

_____

At recess we _____

_____

Things I remember about my first school _____

_____

_____

_____

_____

_____

_____

_____

_____

My secondary school was _____

We wore _____

_____

My favorite subjects were _____

_____

My favorite teachers were _____

_____

Our school colors were _____

Our mascot was _____

Prizes were awarded for _____

_____

At lunchtime I _____

_____

Sports I played at school _____

_____

Clubs I belonged to _____

_____

Special positions I held _____

_____

_____

MY TEENAGE YEARS

When I was a teenager my family lived _____

_____

My ambitions _____

_____

_____

In my spare time I _____

_____

_____

On weekends I _____

_____

_____

My best friends were _____

_____

I liked to spend money on _____

_____

_____

My money came from _____

_____

The fashion rage was _____

_____

_____

What I remember about boyfriends _____

_____

_____

_____

_____

Things that used to make me happy _____

_____

_____

_____

Things that used to upset me _____

_____

_____

After I finished school _____

_____

_____

_____

THINGS I LIKED BEST

My favorite:

Record _____

Singer _____

Actor _____

Actress _____

Play or film _____

Radio or television program _____

_____

Book _____

Sport _____

Activity _____

Food _____

Drink _____

Season _____

Color _____

Holiday _____

Fashion _____

Flower _____

*photograph of
your grandfather*

OUR GRANDFATHER'S YOUTH

Grandfather was born:

Date _____

Place _____

His full name _____

His family lived _____

_____

His parents' jobs _____

_____

_____

He went to school _____

_____

_____

His hobbies were _____

_____

_____

His ambitions were _____

_____

_____

WHEN I MET YOUR GRANDFATHER

Grandfather and I met _____

_____

_____

My age _____

His age _____

Our first date was _____

_____

_____

I liked him because _____

_____

He said he liked me because _____

_____

We liked to go _____

_____

_____

We decided to get married _____

_____

_____

*photograph of
our wedding*

Our wedding

Your grandfather and I were married:

Date _____

Place _____

He wore _____

His best man was _____

His ushers were _____

_____

I wore _____

_____

My flowers were _____

My maid of honor was _____

My bridesmaids were _____

_____

They wore _____

_____

I was given away by _____

*photograph of reception
or honeymoon*

Our wedding reception was held at _____

_____

Number of guests _____

Our favorite wedding present was _____

_____

_____

The things I remember most clearly about the day _____

_____

_____

_____

For our honeymoon we _____

_____

_____

_____

Our First Years Together

When we were first married, your grandfather and I lived in _____
_____
_____

We lived there for _____

Things I liked and disliked about our first home _____
_____
_____
_____

Your grandfather's job was _____
_____

I spent my time _____
_____
_____

In the evenings and on weekends we liked to _____
_____
_____
_____
_____

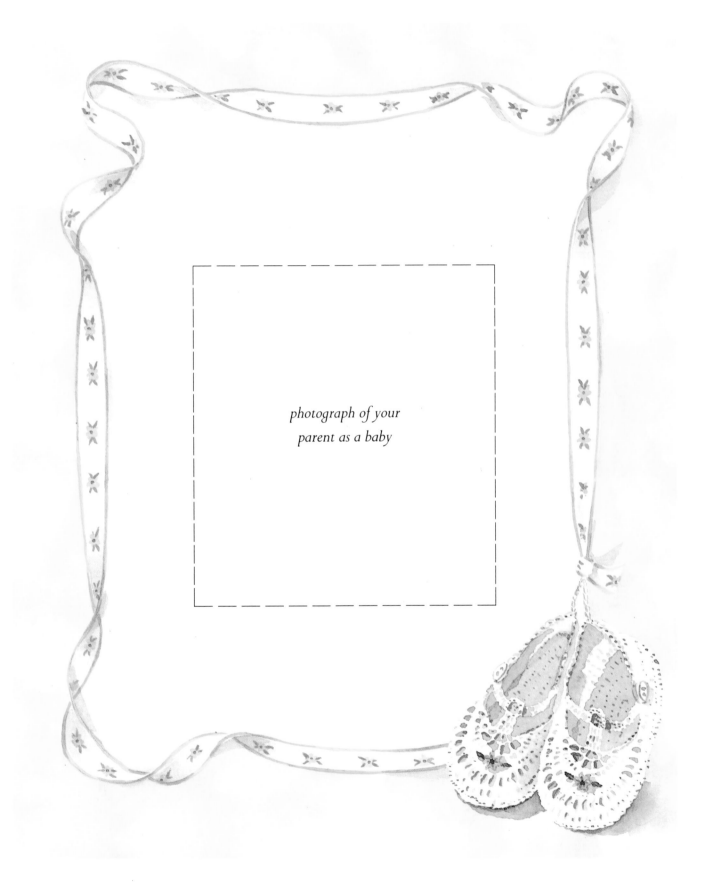

*photograph of your
parent as a baby*

YOUR PARENT WAS BORN

Your parent was born:

Date _____

Place _____

Full name _____

Color of hair at birth _____

Weight at birth _____

We thought our baby looked like _____

_____

Favorite toy _____

First word _____

Nickname _____

Childhood quirks _____

_____

_____

Brothers and sisters _____

_____

_____

_____

*Y*OUR PARENT'S CHILDHOOD

Elementary school _____

Secondary school _____

Best subject in school _____

_____

Interests and hobbies _____

_____

_____

Favorite activities _____

_____

Ambitions _____

_____

Favorite music _____

_____

Favorite fashion _____

_____

Favorite sport _____

We were strict about _____

_____

photograph of
your parents'
wedding

OUR PARENTS

Your mother and father met _____

_____

_____

_____

They were married

Date _____

Place _____

Time _____

The reception was held at _____

_____

_____

For their honeymoon they _____

_____

_____

What I remember best about the day _____

_____

_____

_____

*photograph of
you as a baby*

YOU WERE BORN

You were born:

Date _____

Time _____

Place _____

You weighed _____

When I heard the news I _____

_____

_____

I first saw you _____

_____

_____

_____

My first thoughts about you were _____

_____

_____

_____

_____

$\mathcal{Y}$OUR GRANDMOTHER TODAY

My interests and hobbies _____

_____

_____

_____

Things I like about life today _____

_____

_____

_____

Things I dislike about life today _____

_____

_____

_____

Things I regret _____

_____

_____

Things I still hope to do _____

_____

_____

$\mathcal{T}$HINGS I LIKE BEST TODAY

My favorite:

Music _____

Television program _____

Radio program _____

Actor _____

Actress _____

Entertainer _____

Film _____

Book _____

Food _____

Drink _____

Fashion _____

Color _____

Vacation spot _____

Activity _____

Time of day _____

Season _____

Flower _____

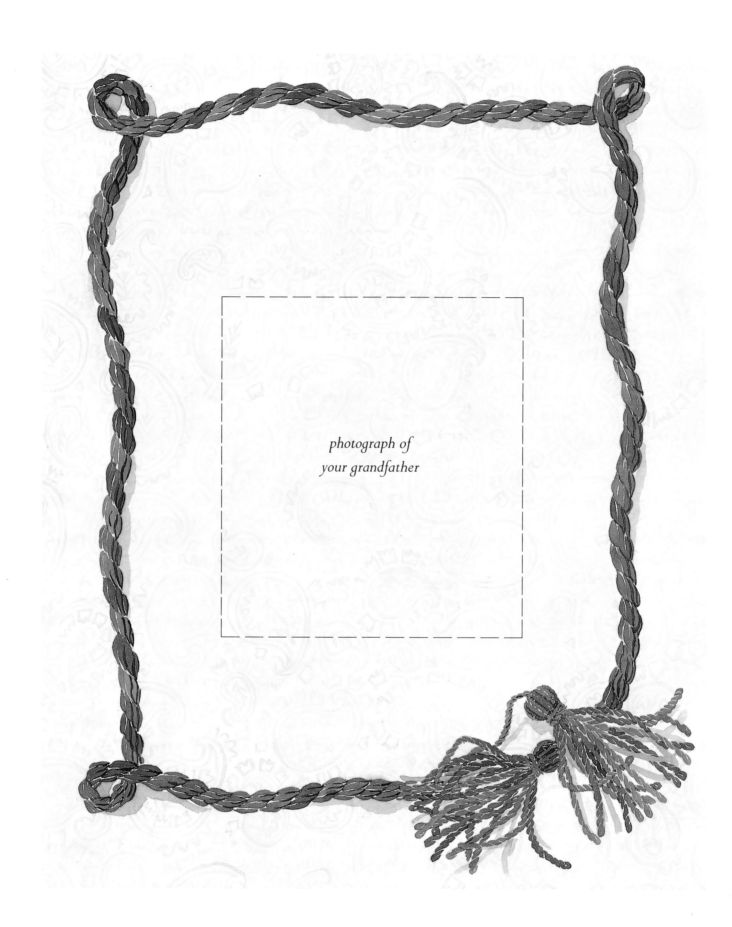

*photograph of
your grandfather*

ALL ABOUT YOUR GRANDFATHER

His job _____

_____

_____

His ambitions _____

_____

_____

His interests and hobbies _____

_____

His friends _____

_____

His likes and dislikes _____

_____

His favorite sport _____

_____

His favorite food and drink _____

_____

His favorite activity _____

_____

THEN AND NOW

How the world has changed since I was a girl:

Inventions _____

_____

_____

Discoveries _____

_____

_____

Attitudes to money _____

_____

Attitudes to women _____

_____

Attitudes to children _____

_____

Manners _____

_____

_____

Travel _____

_____

Entertainment _____

_____

_____

Shopping _____

_____

_____

Education _____

_____

_____

Housing _____

_____

_____

Vacations _____

_____

_____

Clothes and hair styles _____

_____

_____

Gadgets _____

_____

$\mathcal{U}$NFORGETTABLE VACATIONS

FAMILY CELEBRATIONS

Festivity _____

Date _____

We celebrate this occasion by _____

_____

_____

The special foods we eat are _____

_____

_____

Festivity _____

Date _____

We celebrate this occasion by _____

_____

_____

The special foods we eat are _____

_____

_____

Festivity _____

Date _____

We celebrate this occasion by _____

_____

_____

_____

The special foods we eat are _____

_____

_____

Festivity _____

Date _____

We celebrate this occasion by _____

_____

_____

_____

The special foods we eat are _____

_____

_____

FAMILY RECIPES

FAMILY RECIPES

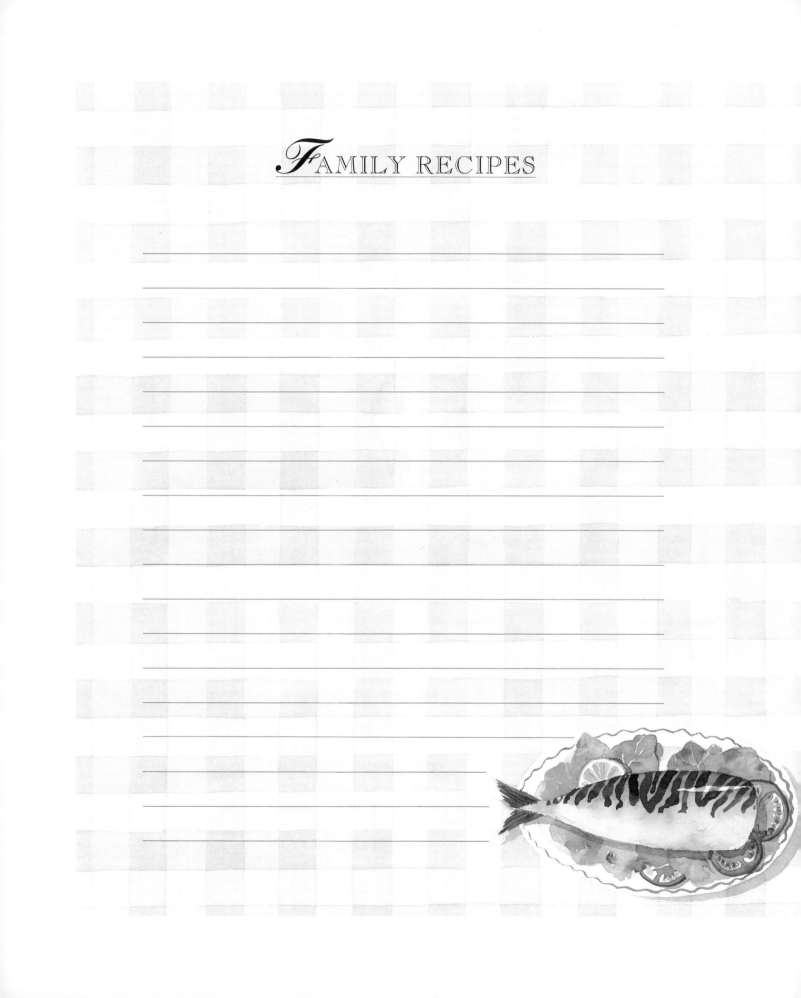

FAMILY ACCIDENTS
AND AILMENTS

_____

_____

_____

_____

_____

_____

_____

_____

_____

_____

_____

_____

_____

_____

_____

_____

_____

$\mathcal{O}$UR RELATIVES

Name _____

Relationship _____

photograph

Name _____

Relationship _____

photograph

Name _____

Relationship _____

photograph

Name _____

Relationship _____

photograph

Name _____

Relationship _____

photograph

Name _____

Relationship _____

photograph

Name _____

Relationship _____

photograph

Name _____

Relationship _____

photograph

NOTES AND PHOTOGRAPHS

NOTES AND PHOTOGRAPHS

NOTES AND PHOTOGRAPHS